Monetized Happiness

Poems from Oakland and San Francisco
by Keith Gaboury

Monetized Happiness
Poems from Oakland and San Francisco
by Keith Gaboury
©2025 Keith Gaboury

Publisher: Duncan Dobson

AMERICAN POETRY SYSTEMS
SOUTH SAN FRANCISCO
CALIFORNIA

www.apsssf.com

Cover image by Duncan Dobson
using Midjourney

APS#008
First Edition
5 4 3 2 1

ISBN 979-8-218-76008-3

Table of Contents

Acknowledgements

Grateful acknowledgements are made to the following publications in which these poems (in some cases, earlier versions and/or different titles) originally appeared:

Beginnings and Endings Anthology (The San Joaquin Valley Writers Branch of the California Writers Club): "You Step into an Oakland Day"

Black Horse Review: "My Egg Choice"

Ginosko Literary Journal: "I Left the Kansas Rectangle," "Tenderloin Bed" (Retitle), and "If Only San Francisco Darkness Had Hands" (Retitle)

GRIFFEL: "Privileged Beauty"

Haight Ashbury Literary Review: "A San Francisco Drive"

Persimmon Review: "When I Dash Across a Don't Walk Intersection"

Poetry Quarterly: Spring 2020: "Cemetery Sky"

The Racket: "Protests Whip Oakland's Bones While I Go Hunting for a Bookshelf Online," "Stray," and "Oakland Eyes"

The Town: An Anthology of Oakland Poets: "Dogs and a Baptist Church," "Lost Cat," and "East Oakland Bus" (Retitle)

The Write Launch: "Transplanted" and "Oakland's Bullet"

Tiny Seed Literary Journal: "In the Smoke"

WordSwell: "Monetized Happiness"

Viewless Wings Poetry Podcast: "One July Ago, There was a Café"

Monetized Happiness

Monetized Happiness

Overlooking unhoused hearts
in a tent encampment,
an East Oakland billboard
zip ties my eyes:
YOU CAN'T BUY HAPPINESS.

Sure, I get it. Then again,
can any vocal cords
vocalize negotiable happiness?

Can we negotiate
a pay-what-you-can happiness
or better yet
a we-need-to-give-a-fuck happiness?

I know I'm Oakland lucky.
I have green
presidents in my pocket
and a lock
on my 38th Avenue door.

When I drop my skin-wrapped
blood onto a $500 mattress
under a $50 blanket
in a square studio
that costs $55 every night,

I dream about burning that billboard
down. A neurological fire
warms my housed blood cells

in this zip code
branded a vegetable desert.
Can I buy a sunny 10¢ carrot

or a joyful $1.50 radish bunch
in my neighborhood
heavy with melanin?

USPS doesn't bother to plant
a dark blue mailbox around here —
doesn't care if I mail a 60¢
envelope of happiness.

I wake up and read
gentrification seeks to swipe away
that tent encampment

for a concrete grocery box
where health and happiness
will be available for purchase
at the checkout counter.

I Hear Oakland Speaking

We walk in May Day sunlight
where Menace barks at a bulldog
chained behind a fence
at the bent junction of Market and 35th.
I pet my twelve-year-old poodle mix.

After he squeezes out a shit ball
under the overpass
of the MacArthur 580,
a woman's unhoused scream
slaps me back into Menace's wet shit.

With my hand gloved
in a plastic bag, I pick up
his black offering,
scrape my boot against a curb.

Surrounded by shopping carts
and engineless cars,
I gape at a mural: two Black kids
stand within a big bloom garden
grinning in their sublime skin.

In the background, a painted home
rattles me like a scream —
their Telegraph Avenue mortgage
surely paid off
and their beds
a clean sheet invitation.

Yet I can't be rooted
in fantasy. We must leave behind
this utopian assault.

Up to 36th and Market,
a driver honks at us
blocking her sharp right turn.
I want to squish her honking
like a stink bug.

Menace growls. He's a compressed
ball of anger. On cracked concrete,
I hear Oakland speaking.

Transplanted

I trip on sidewalk trash
next to an overfilled can
at Ruby and 38th.

In this Mosswood neighborhood,
I pay water and electricity and rent
to breathe in a bedroom
engulfed in white paint
within America's monetized kingdom.

Two blocks away in Mosswood Park,
tents rest supine on city grass
where unhoused hearts vibrate.
Is anyone listening?

A flash of hours ago
when midnight triumphed,
I heard *pop pop pop*
from the privilege of my mattress.

Minutes later, ambulance sirens
shot out like bullets.
Is anyone listening?

At 38th and Ruby
under assaulting sunlight,
I pick my bloody self up
and ask: what if I transplanted myself
into a fern-painted bedroom?

Through a yawning door, I amble
into a backyard fantasy
to plant an appleseed.
Over a cascade of Oakland days,

a sapling bursts through black soil
by the strength of solar kisses.
I swallow a Golden Delicious
under a rooted sky.

A Feathered Divide

Through my living room window, I spot
a peacock resident
prowling Occidental and 61st Street
yet they don't pay a mortgage
or buy a $7 mocha latte.

I must say — their sapphire blue body
and long verdant tail
rejuvenate
Occidental Street
with a douse of untamed colors.

No one can land on a name.
Paul and I toss between
Paco or Peter or Pierre.

Kind reader, can you pluck
one name
from this P-anointed klatch?

I bet Paul is punching
his keyboard now
to post an ALL CAPS tirade online
how his eyelids get pinned open

and he can't dream
any winged dreams
whenever Paco
screeches under a waxing shine.

Oh kindred reader, I didn't
let you pick a name — I hope
you're not mad — I've decided
Oakland's got a Paco peacock.

I sleep one block down — I'm never
waken by any peacock shakes
in an Oakland darkness
that habitually hosts
unhoused lives.

I sip a Monday mocha latte
when Paul thuds on my door.
After I swig one terminus gulp,
I unlock the deadbolt
to hear him declare,

"Let's herd a posse
to snatch that peacock up
and jam it into a pot
for a neighborhood feast."

My kingly reader, would you consume
a peacock stew
with vengeful spices?
I'll never partake.

Out on a Paradise
Park jog, Paco
squawks before an unhoused man
who's trying to run down sleep
on a cracked sidewalk.

I know this man. Ben
was once my neighbor.
I jettison over

where my shadow drapes over him
like a black blanket
on a feral day.

If Only San Francisco Darkness Had Hands

You say now's the time
to squeeze San Francisco
out of our 40-year-old selves.

If our future heartbeats
pump inside a suburban address,
will we still love each other
before mirrors that heave back
unknown reflections?

Will we ever return
to our Inner Richmond neighborhood?
We must shamble down Geary
as aliens who swallow Nizario's Pizza.

You must know
we'll no longer know the special shade
of the Redwood Grove Garden
that wraps around
our weekend bodies.

If only San Francisco darkness had hands,
they could build a 94118-zip-code home
for you, me, and the unborn life you carry.
Our teachers' paychecks just aren't enough.

At our 4th and Clement apartment,
I just installed a new doorbell.
The chime vibrates a welcome
so anyone is invited
to feel my breath and pulse and voice.

Tenderloin Bed

You reach your apartment lock,
open darkness
into your Hyde and Eddy apartment
next to New Princess Market
next to a brain
encased inside a white-knuckle skull
who sleeps within tent walls.
In your spry youth, did you believe
in a princess getting saved by a sober
prince? Another beauty
just ODed on Eddy across from the SFPD.
Four states away, your mom's
comatose body
occupies a hospital room.
You sprawl across your bed
where you slip into a sleep
not fixed to a ventilator
or on a concrete mattress.

Look Out! for Stampeding Rain

After a string of in-heat dog days,
the sky unlatches
their cloud gate,

lets loose a raining kennel
of cats and dogs
clawing my face raw.

I sprint through this stampede
south of Golden Gate Park
within a grid

I'm lucky to have
a mailing address in, lucky
like an immunized fox
with all their shots.

With a prick and a Band-Aid,
I got my flu shot yesterday.
I'm now shielded
against a viral rampage.

Band-Aid in the trash,
I kick Sam's cavernous dog bowl
in an apartment I pay rent
and half my heart to occupy.

Yet for how long?
I'm between jobs
like I'm between lives.

Grandpa Charlie once told me
under a grinning lamplight
I'll be reincarnated
as a concrete dweller.

When my next-life heartbeats
vibrate in my next-life body,
I'll still have to knife over
next-life rent
or be left to rot

like Sam
who got crushed by a steel cage
that sped through
a sunrise traffic light.

When A San Francisco Wind Shoved Me Back

on 7th Avenue
like a 7th grade bully,
a mind in the wind
flung my flimsy self about.
I still lurched forward
a block from Golden
Gate Park's
shuddering leaves.
I can't remember:
did I stumble
through an infant
morning's crawling sunrays
caught in a kidnapping wind
or trudge through
a windstorm day
gaping
through cataractic
eyes of dusk?
My memory
is blowing away
like a balloon
untethered
to a California hand.
Since a windy wind goes so very windy,
does a mind
shaken by a wind shove
go mendy
not to be mixed up
with my neighbor Mindy
who lives with her senior
cat Maureen
and trails of shedding fur?
At 7th and Cabrillo,
I saw my one
and only Misty

draped in a misty veneer.
Are mist and wind friends?
I admit this mist
might be a fiction
camped
in my married mind.
Oh I remember now
the age of that day:
we got wind-slapped
in a wrinkled windy day.
Stamped
with a time of sunset death,
this sunlight got reborn
into a newborn night
as we dipped
our mendy minds
into Safeway's glow
to seek out marmalade
we soon spread
across sour-
dough of calm.
The wind's feet
stomped
on the trail home
past Maureen's
abandoned fur.
Back in our walled
escape, after we witnessed
Mindy snatch out
her bedroom light,
Misty swallowed a sweet
spread
within our windless
haven.

An Oakland Aubade

Our eyes snap open
into the shards of a shattered night
after sleep nested
on our branch bodies.
Outside our open
bedroom glass, Black-Crowned
Night-Herons
chirp in their familial nest.
While we lie entangled
on our queen bed
in a clean sheet union,
my ears rattle
when a homeless man's moaning
trounces the papa heron

squawking into a weekend dawn.

Mere feet from the frame
we pay a property
tax to occupy,
when will he return to his rotten nest
down the block!?
Oh his moaning is marring
our Oakland repose.
With our need
for scrambled eggs, you spring
up and wing
across the floor
like a monarch butterfly.
You glide
within our salaried kingdom.

A Lake Merritt Nocturne

Beside lapping water,
I wander
along Lakeshore Avenue.

When a passing poodle yelps,
I'm startled out of my stupor

within a black pool
between lampposts aglow.

Opposite the Cleveland Cascade
still holding the echo
of a cascading flow,

a giant sequoia
sings a ballad.
I stop and listen.

Night grows
into the wet company

of chattering roots
under my Oakland feet.

Complicit

I slurp coffee with cream
on a Lake Merritt bench
across from waters
flowing like imported coffee
into commuting mouths.

Shit. Underpaid or unpaid hands
surely plucked these Columbian coffee beans
that gives my American brain
such a sweet caffeinated kick.

Once I jolt up in denim jeans,
I spring back to the MADE IN CHINA tag
I spotted this morning
when I grabbed them
crumpled off the floor.

Shit. Underpaid or unpaid hands
surely stitched these jeans
that drape my American legs.

On Grand Avenue, I fall
into Clio's Bookstore. On a shelf
fused with I bet imported wood,
I snatch a book on globalization.

At checkout, I get a free bookmark
and a free smile for buying local.

Shit. The sales tax I just paid
will help bankroll
the genocide in Gaza.
There's no payment in death.

Clutching my paperback,
I sprint back to Lake Merritt
where I lean over the edge
to gape at my American reflection.

I'm lucky to still own
a heartbeat.

Oakland's Bullet

When Oakland took their bullet
for a walk, that runaway caliber
pressed its width into brown skin

within a multigenerational neighborhood
outsiders stamp as another ghetto.
Oakland took their bullet for a jog

to shake off the residue
of last night's murder.
A brown skin boy

I knew since he drank orphaned milk
got his dinner removed
after Oakland took their bullet for a sprint

through screams bouncing from a jungle
gym open from dawn to dusk.
A brown skin body lies unheard

in an autopsy room. Oakland
dances with their bullet
while a brown skin family
sleeps with hollow stomachs.

Protests Whip Oakland's Bones While I Go Hunting for a Bookshelf Online

when I come across a commanding one
I bet my books will claim
as their home. In the question section,
a customer asked if this bookshelf
comes armed. Will a sleek

Smith & Wesson
stand as complementary security
to this plywood purchase?
Once I stack

Wright and Baldwin and Ellison together,
I'll be loaded in the barrel
killing America to make a better America.

My five-shelved gun
arrives tomorrow by nightfall. I'll assemble it

as the police station burns.

II

You Step into an Oakland Day

On a neighborhood sidewalk
cracked by finger roots,

I spot you through the MLK Café window
where your feet hook into MLK Way
down the block from Marcus Books.
Have you read any Black
authors this year,
this decade, this century?

You breach MLK Café
to buy your regular black coffee
from a Black woman you've seen
in her employee skin
every workday for the past year.

I smile as if I'm your sister
yet you don't know my name.

My Caffeinated Isolation

I drink coffee
like I breathe oxygen.
To be more tablespoon exact,

I breathe oxygen
like I gulp pumpkin
spiced lattes in November

when slapping rains
imprison me
into a solitary fish
in the fishbowl of my apartment.

In July, I inhale ice
white mochas
when the sun flips everything
into a rent-controlled sauna.

On this January day
when the new year
is still fresh and clean, I brew
a new pot with caramel grains

and pour this hot gold
into my insulated cup.
I live an insulated life

but I must propel
out my Grand Lake door
into an anxiety pool

along Lake Merritt's
polluted reflection.
How many finned friendships
inhabit below the surface?

I'm stirring my new year resolution
to brew a new friendship
between every month's
waxing and waning glows.

Can I light up a conversation
with a striped bass
or longjaw mudsucker?

I haven't had any success
with the human kind.

Yet on a black bench, I spot
a man sipping coffee
in a turtleneck
as I sip my own caramel kick.

I trudge forward
in the shield of a leatherback shell.
Before the bench, I stop

where my words
pour out
like spilled coffee.

One July Ago, there was a Café
at Broadway and Grand
yet its name just leaped
off my tongue
like my great-uncle Gary
who leaped off the Golden Gate Bridge
to his Pacific Ocean coffin.
They never found his body
like I can't find the name
of that Grand Avenue café.
On a grand ultraviolet day,
its walls got smashed
by a wrecking ball.
Before they flipped over
their 'CLOSED' sign
for the terminus time, I stood
in a café line
that pays a property tax
to occupy my memory
where I picked up offshoots
of a conversation
like how Gary
picked me up in his gray pickup truck
at the Amtrak station on 2nd and Alice.
He smiled with such unshackled joy
as he drove through a rainstorm.
In the café line, I remember
these big fat raindrops
muscled themselves down to the ground
as one friend said to the other:
"Did you hear they just put a net
around the Golden Gate Bridge
to catch anyone trying to commit suicide?"
I itched to jumpstart a suicide
from the café line
when an employee, a savior
with coffee-black hair,

ushered me forward
with a midday whistle.
Yesterday I saw this employee
unemployed and unhoused
next to the Starbucks on Clay.
After I dropped them a silver dollar,
I ambled home under a silver moon
round like a noose.

When I Dash Across a Don't Walk Intersection

at 40th and Broadway, Death's
warm body almost hugs me

as a SUV almost flattens me
into one of Mama's blueberry pies

hot from a Thanksgiving oven
three decades ago

and it's still steaming somewhere
within my cluttered hippocampus.

At 40th and Broadway, thankfully
I'm not a blueberry pie.

According to Consciousness
as illuminated by my high school

guidance counselor, I'm alive —
yet do I deserve to be?

Thirty Thanksgivings ago,
Papa cut into a blueberry pie

a week after Aunt Mary's neck
snapped. Now I dive

into Mama's Royal Café.
With a smack

of crimson lipstick, a waitress
nods one greasy hello.

"A slice of blueberry pie, please."
"We're all out, hun."

"Just give me all the blue-
berries you have.

I'll flatten them
like a SUV squishing a brain."

My Egg Choice

White or brown?
If my white skin picks white eggs,
surely I'm suffering
an historical flare-up
to America's racial flavor.
Between caged and free-
range brown, I grab
the $5.99 free-range.
I'm looking to eat
eggs born from unshackled mothers.

Out of Duboce Triangle's Safeway,
I trot across Market, skip down Dolores.
All the while, I clutch my egg choice
like twelve brown babies.
Yet as I leap over Muni tracks,
a M train nearly squishes me
and my babies. I escape
with all twelve yolks
still encased
within their proud brown shells.

At home, I open the egg
carton's confinement
to crack three into a black skillet
and gobble up my babies
I once protected as a parent
now scrambled in a free-range
rapture hot on a plate.
Nestled in yellow,
a small brown shell
gapes at my breakfast eyes.

Breakfast at Hamburger Haven

A week after the Apollo 11 landing,
I sip a fresh pour of coffee
before my scrambled eggs and toast

among a line of Saturday customers
at the shared countertop.
Barbara, a regular

who holds a strawberry jam bottle
with stories
in her hands, asks,

"Do you need the jam?
I don't want to hog it."
A chuckle bounces out.

When I mutter,
"Oh no thank you,"
she answers with a grin,
"My Pa had a sweet tooth.
He slathered jam on his toast."

Spinning her barstool
to fully face my Irish features,
she studies me
like a lunar rock.

"You look like a friend I knew
in Dachau. Paul.
His name was Paul."

Back at Hamburger Haven
one Saturday later, Barbara yells
across the countertop:

"Paul! Remember me?
How did you survive Dachau?
My Ma and Pa didn't."

Once I wave over my chilled water,
I scoop out an ice cube
to crush its lunar crater coldness
between my back molars.

An egg sizzles on the fryer.
With a wink on the side,
the dish slides
before Barbara's tattooed smile.

Cemetery Run

Mary runs through the open gate
of Mountain View Cemetery

where gravestones surround
her sweat on a curved road.

In Mountain View, she gapes
upon a downtown skyline.

Stopping on a curved road,
cemetery roses make her shiver.

Sprinting on, she glares upon Downtown
Oakland vaulting into a commercial sky

spliced from this cemetery sky
that hosts rose petals crumbling like concrete.

Mary wants to shake out this sky's sorrow.
Gravestone names

mark where bones crumble
within coffin darkness.

Gravestone names
surround her eyes

over coffin darkness.
Mary runs into an open sky.

A Zombie in Mountain View Cemetery

Under an onion moon
sliced into an Oakland sky,
I move within the skin
of an *Evil Dead* zombie

across mummy brown soil.
My brain is rolled tight
like a papyrus scroll
before Uncle Kevin's tombstone.

A Frankenstein stroll away
from his White House bones,
his wife sleeps
in a hospital comatose.

I'm ready to be comatosed
within another b-horror marathon.
Before I grab fresh snacks
at S-Mart in the next breathless week,

I'll search for a young
Bruce Campbell
gripping a chainsaw
under a lemon sun.

Sienna's Walk

An Oakland night
shimmies down daylight's throat
as I anchor my ten-pound terrier
Sienna to a brown leash.

Out the door on Pleasant
Valley Avenue, we amble
on cracked concrete, concrete

Uncle Kevin poured
ten springs ago
sliced between his whiskey and smoking
consumption.

We brisk through two crosswalks
and swing onto Piedmont Avenue.
Within sprinting distance
is Piedmont Café

where Kevin used to slip inside
for coffee and a pancake stack
after he tossed his smoke to the curb.

While Sienna's alabaster fur
absorbs a wind shove,
we lock sight before the locked gate

of Mountain View Cemetery.
Seven years on,
Kev is consumed in soil.

On an incline, grass pumps up
over his collapsed
heartbeat.

Dogs and a Baptist Church

populate my north Oakland neighborhood
where I habitually walk my rat terrier
Batman and his spiky ears
in still-forming dawns.

Last week, as we slid past
a locked gate at 37th and West,
a Rottweiler barked up against the metal
as if we aimed
to torpedo her home.

I jumped, my city stupor
shaken into Sunday morning fear
while Batman's tiny black body
growled right back.
I've never seen him murder a rat
but he has the teeth for it.

Down another block
at Market and 37th, I prepared
for a pit bull behind a fence
to bark out a litany of anger.
Instead, they sat back, gaping
from their grassless reality.

As we looped back home, a gospel
escaped from the 37th Street Baptist Church.
Batman yelped out a shot of pleasure
into our 9:00 AM air.

Lost Cat

I read my horoscope in coffee grains.
With my pulverized future
in my denim pocket, I go out walking.

At West and 37th, in front of Spokeland,
I spot a lost cat poster
pinned to a street pole
like another messiah I don't believe in.

More than the holes
in a crucified man's hands,
I've come to worship
a caffeinated spike.

I slurp back my religion
as I stare into this cat's
gemstone eyes: I know this feline —
his name is Jose.

My girlfriend Brittany
claimed him last Easter
after his stray fur
darted into a dirty Lake Merritt.

On a Good Friday
now dead to me, I snuggled with Jose
when Brittany declared, "We're done."
I must say she's my ex.

Now I can reclaim Jose as my own.
I'll search for him on 37th,
trudge up MLK Way,
saunter along Telegraph.

If I fail to find him in Temescal,
I'll abandon my coffee grain horoscope
next to Church's Texas Chicken.

The neon 'OPEN' sign
always greases my eyes
when I step inside with a feline smile.

Standing Before North Oakland Colors

Through a glass divide,
I love when you watch me
walk onto the sidewalk
before our 45th and Market home.

By my early morning side, Zeus
and his terrier ears
poke into an Oakland sky
where clouds ascend into a new day.

As I halt at our neighbor's wood fence
and relish upon
the lavender and iris and hyacinth
purple flowers,

I remember
when we exhaled college breaths,
Professor Simpson lectured

how Heracles and his dog
once walked across a storytelling beach.
I still imagine the strength
of each Heraclean footfall
puffing up a sandy cloud.

Once his dog bit into a sea snail
and Tyrian purple blood
squirted out, Heracles

knelt down to gaze upon
his pet's mouth painted in blood
from either a cut or kill.

How did Heracles wash away
that blood? If I spotted Zeus
with a blood-drenched mouth,
I'd jet over to the vet
at Shattuck and 45th.

With my pudgy stomach and stick muscles,
I know I'm not Heracles.
Why do you still love me?

Back at home after a loop
to MLK Way, Zeus barks hello
as your DIY smile
hurries a greeting.

Laundry must be divided by color —
dust bunnies euthanized — Zeus' processed
breakfast dumped into his bowl.

Before all that, I hug you.
We're not living in mythology.

III

A San Francisco Drive

Scarlet horsepowers
crimson command on California 1
while bodies, scorched by a UV tongue,
lounge on Pacific Ocean sand
where tan lines grow
into cancer's waiting room.
Back in a decade now dead,
Scarlet slept on that same
red punishment
until Dr. Baskind
cut out a mole's malpractice.
With lipstick pop and cayenne hair,
a vermillion skirt
drapes over a scar
welded into skin
as Scarlet hurls down
that concrete red carpet
next to a maroon minivan
where a sunburnt child
licks strawberry ice cream
first scooped
over at Hometown Creamery.
At a screaming stoplight,
crimson and maroon break
for a woman, born ruby cheeked
under a blood
transfusion moon,
grips a cherry leash
fixed to an Irish Setter's chestnut neck.
When they walk across the walkway,
an apartment fire
button-down
blazes a confidence of warmth
before Scarlet's hooked eyes.

Within My Body's Garden

Tonight I'll sleep
in perennial growth
with a freshly bought amaranth
sprouting on my bedside pine.
First, I must grow a friendship
with my neighbor Berry.

We live on Chester Avenue
along a street of two-story houses,
tree lined with mirror front yards
on the southern sliver of San Francisco.

Whenever Berry spots my resident frame
on a sidewalk
or the sidewalk that vines
to the adult movie theater
in Stonestown, his mouth cyclically
sprouts a smile.

I've decided: I'll bake him an amaranth
velvet cake. As I'm mixing
the dough, I drop in a few blood drops
like the Aztecs did
so many seasons ago. The Aztecs
didn't own an ancient Kitchen Aid —
Berry's cake is born faster.

As our feet grip Chester concrete
under a flower vase streetlight,
I hand him my red delight —
my bandaged ring finger exposed —
oh he smiles a jungle,
a jungle gym of happiness.

Back home, after I water
my bedside companion, I prepare for sleep.
Surely Berry will smile anew
in my rooted dream.
I want him, I need him
to plant an amaranth seed
within my body's garden.

In Queen Cleo's Kingdom

My neighbor Cleo
is the reincarnated Cleopatra.
Do you believe me?
Surely you believe me. Cleo

possesses the same curly
black hair, aquiline nose,
and skin the same shade
of a newborn dusk.

Then there's her week-old son!
Alexander's vine curls
swirl like strawberry vines.
He's the heir-in-waiting

in Queen Cleo's Kingdom
on Chester Avenue
where suburban houses
plop one after the other.

At the curve of Chester and Payson,
Cleo's burgundy mansion
sits in high sunshine glory.
I'm right next door oh so close

to royalty. Whenever I hold a blink
for a hundred heartbeats, I imagine
Alexander swaddled in Cleo's arms
as he swallows her breast milk

white like marble. I'll be a mother
by the next waxing crescent.
If I must, I'll borrow Alexander
for a day or a week or a year.

Once she pushed her stroller
back home this morning, I spotted
her approach and sprinted out past
my neighbor Berry eating a cranberry.

"Greetings my Queen. Alexander
is so gorgeous. I just want to eat him up
like a ripe strawberry." Queen Cleo spoke
in her monarch tongue, "I'm not your queen!

I'm Cleo! Stay away from my son!"
She sought to stress my loyalty
as I threaded a sight on her jar
of saffron threads. "My Queen,

where did you acquire
your glorious saffron?"
"Did you hear me?
I'm not your queen!

I'm Cleo! and I'm going to take
a saffron bath to get away from you."
"Yes, Cleopatra
enjoyed saffron soaks just like you."

At dusk, I strut past my bedroom bookshelf
stuffed with Cleopatra books
to stand naked on bathroom tiles

before saffron threads sprinkled on top
of bathtub water. Yesterday,
Doctor Baskind forced upon me
a child of dead language: "You can't conceive."

Now I'll be reincarnated
a mother to-be
when I submerge my womb
into saffron's crimson power.

Fever through Time

If you and your fever
existed in the European
Middle Ages,

you would have ingested
a dose of lapis lazuli pigment
to cure your ailment.
That's how the thinking went.

Oh you'd better get ready
for an exorcism
if you perspired
in ancient Mesopotamia.

What if you lived
with a Roman Empire fever
in a past life?

You must have pleased the deities
who made you sick
by placing amulets
in the Temple of Febris.

In a young February morning,
you rush your 100°F self
under bloodstained clouds
to the CVS opening its jaw

doors at 5th and Lincoln
across from Golden Gate Park's
cypress tree wall.

You stumble in your sweltering skin
down aisle 3. Before a blur
of pill bottles, you blurt out,

"Where the hell is the Tylenol?"
like a 9th-century man with a fever like you
wondering where his lapis lazuli
went hiding.

I Stride with My Gut Flora

through the Rose Garden
on Funston Avenue's concrete path
tucked within Golden
Gate Park's nature metropolis.

Oh this flora of rosebuds
mirror the gut flora
of viruses, fungi, and bacteria
inhabiting my digestive tract
as permanent residents.

I read or at least I think I read
one's gut flora
weighs the same as a hamster.

At home, it's feeding time.
Once I text Samantha
to satisfy Marshmallow
in her hamster cage,

I stop to inhale a splash
of San Francisco air. I don't know
the names of these rosebuds

like I don't know
the names of the flowers
splattered around our apartment.
Samantha planted each one.
So why should I learn?

Up to Fulton Street, I wait
for the next outbound 5 bus.
After 500 seconds

or the time it takes Samantha
to yank up a string of backyard weeds,
a 5 bus halts, jolts its doors open.

How many hamster
viruses are waiting
for me inside?

I sit beside a man in a flower shirt.
As he streams his hair back,
the bus streams past The Floral Loft.
Samantha is poking us to go
to their going-out-of-business sale.

When I tumble home,
Samantha prods me,
"Water the blood
orange roses" but I don't know
where the oranges live.

Instead, I let Marshmallow
out of her cage to scamper about
in a shallow pocket
of Ocean Beach sunlight.

I must swing back
to the Rose Garden tomorrow.
In a freshly planted sunrise, I hope
Samantha and Marshmallow
will join my gut flora and me.

Pink Behavior

On Good Friday, I wolfed down
God-worthy pizza. Pizza gives me heartburn.
Still, I worshiped every
mozzarella and pepperoni bite

at our 2nd Street apartment.
Three-hundred square feet
squeezes me from all sides.

At our table, Mary
sliced through my devotion
when she spat out,

"You chew too loudly!"
as she cooked me
with her oven eyes.

A hungry thought
tried to push my right fist
to plant a black eye on her
like Ash Wednesday ashes.
I halted myself

yet I needed to escape
so I called my tattooed friend
Mark who lives on Clement
above Green Apple Books.

In a CVS aisle
with pepperoni breath,
I stood surrounded
by the lure of medicating away
my burning heart.

Before the Pepto-Bismol,
Mark soothes me a story:
after a Washington State prison
painted a cell

that Pepto-Bismol shade,
the prisoner's rapid aggression
plunged to a calm heart rate.

"Is that all it takes?" I asked him.
Mark displayed his Gemini
constellation tattoo
blazing across his forearm.
"Hell if I know, John.
You should ask the stars."

At checkout, I bought a pink bottle
and a green apple
with a sticker
labeled like my black eye marriage.

On a Geary sidewalk
where streetlights
muscled out starlight,
I threw back a pink shot
and said with a chuckle,

"Hey Mark, this better cure
my heartburn and marriage.
That prisoner got surrounded by pink.
I'm now pink on the inside."

Cochineal Vengeance

In her strawberry red lipstick,
Scarlet struts into Carmine
Organic Foods, a red edifice
that financially kisses
Bernal Heights' neighborhood mouth
with non-GMO lips.

Straight to ice cream indulgence,
she stands before a slate of frozen flavors.
Once Scarlet clutches a strawberry offering,
she spots under the ingredients list
Natural Red No. 4.

Hoarding all the red pints she can clutch
in her San Francisco arms,
she propels toward the exit
when a high schooler with a flimsy name tag
halts her in her cold tracks.

"You have to pay for those."
"What's natural about killing
innocent insects? Oh you're too young to know."

She sprints out onto Bocana Street.
Would you? The minimum wage kid
yelps after her
as she juggles her cold grift
down to Cortland Avenue

and into Succulence, a plant nursery
birthing priced vegetation.
Among a blooming color spectrum,

Scarlet opens a pint
dyed by smashing cochineal insects
who once crawled on Peruvian cacti.
She rubs her pilfered ice cream
hard across a cactus' bristles. Would you?

"You contaminated that cactus
with ice cream! You must pay for it!"
an employee commands
in her auburn authority shirt and lips.

"I put these lucky cochineal
back where they belong! They were slaugh-
tered for strawberry ice cream!
By the way, your red lipstick
got dyed with cochineal."

With Scarlet's right hand a red smear,
she builds a structurally unstable
Golden Gate smile. Would you?

East Oakland Bus

At MacArthur and Maple
across from Diamond Market
where the beer and smokes
preach my name, I jam myself
onto a 57 outbound
within a swath of wedged bodies.
On a seat for a human
pregnant, disabled or senior,
you — with spry skin,
no pregnancy or limp —
flick on a lighter
to speed your fingers
through the red tip.
Passengers swerve
compressed stares away
when your thumbprint
singes black. The driver
steers under a green light
as you mercifully
kill that burn.
The front doors swing open
at the MacArthur and 35th stop
for your limbs to tumble out.
You left your lighter
on the seat. A pregnant
woman now sits there.
I slide open a window
to fling your flame
out onto Oakland concrete.

Downtown Dust

As I transverse across
the 20th and Broadway walkway,
construction dust
from the rat nest
of a growing tower
scurries into my lungs.
This will be luxury living
not built for pay like mine.
I cough a wallop
yet a dusty rat
still feeds on me.

Down the 19th Street
BART stairs, I nearly crush
a pigeon who flaps away
into a cerulean sky escape.
The rat in my lungs
won't scamper away
as I squeeze myself
onto a southbound train
away from the borders
of my birth, borders
I no longer love.

In the Smoke

"The Camp Fire started on Thursday, November 8, 2018, in
Northern California's Butte County . . . an urban firestorm formed in
the foothill town of Paradise."

Smoke sweeps down Oakland sidewalks
in the skin of a climate killer
ravaging lungs.

Inside Pete's Coffee on Lakeshore,
a woman says to her friend,

"The smoke no longer carries
burnt bodies
from the people of Paradise."

Around noon, the Camp Fire
moved on to the forest
that once hugged the town
now aflame on TV and phone screens.

"It's better to breathe burnt trees
than burnt bodies, right?"

I flip on my face mask,
exit the cafe into a haze
past Grand Lake neighbors with only
their eyes in sight.

At home on Rand Avenue, I welcome indoor air
when the couple I rent from
stumbles in through the back door.

They take off their masks,
inhale the clean.

"Hey, do you wanna share a smoke?"
David asks. "Yeah. I just bought a pack,"
Beth answers with a smile.

In the doorway, she leans outside
to strike a match.

In the Colors

Behind red brake lights —
we stop

and then speed under a green
stoplight toward firelight

within sunlight
infected

by all this smoke
bombarding

San Francisco zip codes —
the radio flares an update —

"the Camp Fire now burns
the town of Paradise" —

we cut into the Presidio —
stop

within a chlorophyll
assault —

through our window view
we finally see bits of tree green —

what are we doing —
peace fled to a hideout —

this smoke smothers
the international orange

that coats
the Golden Gate Bridge —

this smoke
of televised engulfment —

screamless bodies —
charred heart tissue

ensnares us
inside a chamber —

this smoke
wraps a bone

white blanket
over our eyes —

Six Ways of Looking at a Sunflower
After Wallace Stevens

Within a wash of chlorophyll
on a spine path in Joaquin Miller Park,
we stand before

a cluster of sunflowers:
golden yellow petals
confident in their own shade.

●

Vine back to a pre-Contact
sunrise. An indigenous palm
planted a sunflower seed
into mummy brown soil

where the MacArthur 580
cuts like a blade
across enslaved skin.

●

When cosmetics
squeeze out sunflower seeds,
the extracted oil
gives your Oakland skin
a fresh sheen

when you plant your feet
before Van Gogh's sunflowers
growing on a de Young Museum Wall
within Golden Gate Park.

●

You claim your Grandpa Charlie
drove west to California
on an engine
powered by sunflower oil.

•

When a Mammoth Russian Sunflower
climbs fourteen feet
in our engineered
Oakland Hills garden,

your sunburnt neck
twists to witness
a pollinating skyscraper's
command.

•

I love
how you cooked
last night's anniversary dinner
with sunflower oil
in the frying pan.

Privileged Beauty

When a white popping sky
buckles stars into constellations off a blacktop road,
I ask my mind: how many can't see redshift starlight
as they breathe behind twenty-five-to-life metal

      or beneath a roof of buckling pollution?
      After I read and wrote and screamed, it's time
      I breathe — claim my Milky Way view
      like the currency in my pocket.

My white self reads an author who doesn't mirror my melanin.
Yesterday at dusk on a hotel bed, I visualized
pickpocketing America's fat body — dead
presidents got thrown into a furious fire.

      On this bed I paid to occupy, I'll dream a new reality
      where my son's heartbeats vibrate in a zip code
      that won't throw his chambers into a cell or casket.
      Photons within one galactic neighborhood

pour into our terrestrial home of heartbeats
and gunshots. How many can't see shifting beauty,
only know horror in a neighborhood with prison bars?
Tonight I gazed at a California sky's familiar shine.

IIII

Oakland Bloodletting

Behind our Adams Point home,
on the mowed grass
where we pay property tax
for each square footage,

I stand among a blooming
multiverse of pollination.
Next to my Night Sky Petunias,
my Chocolate Cosmos flowers
swirl alive

yet I can't get lost in all this growth —
our mortgage is due
and I must buy new fertilizer —

yet each Chocolate Cosmos
possesses wondrously
deep crimson petals.

What if we lived on Mayan
pre-conquered land
among an outpouring
of Chocolate Cosmos
that mirrored native blood?

They paid a bloodletting debt
back to the Mayan Gods
who birthed the universe.
I surely would have fallen
into the bloodletting line.

Yesterday I paid off our credit
card debt. Did I pay back
the American Credit God?

Back when your O+ pints
oxygenated your teenage body,
did your flower tattoo bleed
for style or a bloodletting debt?

Once you shuffle back inside,
I watch you slice up
a beef sacrifice for our supper.

At our dead tree table,
we salivate over a cooked carcass
with two glasses of merlot
in the colonized world
we were born into.

At the San Francisco Flower Market

On a too-hot Mother's Day,
I'm shopping for you.
In the Neve Brothers line,

I spot ruby red magnolias,
sulfur yellow daisies, and bronze petal
black-eyed Susans

when I lurch back three decades
to when you married
a man's sapphire gaze.

On that night
crowded with white knuckle icicles,
a post-honeymoon punch

populated your left eye
into an obsidian
shade of pain.

I still remember your scream
spreading like a weed
I couldn't stop.

Through a screen door,
his black boulder stare
thudded toward me.

Under the florist's glare,
a man in a 49ers sweater
and a woman sipping Pete's Coffee

all wait behind me
with a plucked impatience.
I must decide. At last,

I buy a dozen black-eyed Susans.
Sweating outside at 6th and Brannan,
I drive south to Esprit Park

where I know you'll be waiting
with an empty vase
and a sprouting smile.

You Left the Kansas Rectangle

three presidents ago
yet you still have
a 913 Kansas area code.

On a ripe Saturday
at the Ferry Plaza Farmers Market,
you smile with an out-of-state mouth.

As you bite
into a Central Valley strawberry,
your phone screams.

I hear you welcome
your father's voice. He's standing
before his Kansas window.

Watermelon Reveal

In a museum's ticketed room,
I saunter through
an overload of framed color

until I stand transfixed
before 17th-century watermelons
painted by Giovanni Stanchi:

there's that signature green rind
yet a knife exposed
black seeds

encased within wheels
of a diluted red
surrounded by white streaks.

"What am I looking at?"
I ask my 21st-century self
fixed on San Francisco ground.

I leave the museum's prestige.
Past a klatch
of Market Street melon eaters,

my RGB color cones
latch onto Trader Joe's
crimson sign at 4th and Market.

Out front, I nod
hello to a man
swallowing H_2O.

Straight to those green
globes piled together,
I snatch one

and slam a ripe roundness
against the reflective floor.
A smooth and seedless rupture

reveals an assertive red
splattered before
my art-paying eyes.

Under a Locally Foreign Sky

In Old Oakland,
you transverse
Jefferson and 8th

in the same city
your paycheck gets swallowed
by rent, electricity, and water
to live and read and drink.

How many miles
from this intersection
do you sleep?

On a Jefferson sidewalk block
near Washington Street and MLK Way,
you know these names
but you don't know these streets.

As you wander toward
a cafe haven on 9th, you stare
down at the deity
of your Google Maps's
blue ball tracker

when you trip over
a sleeping man
unhoused
beside Blue Bottle Coffee.

Your right knee's blood
hits 9th and Washington Street air
under a locally foreign sky.

Bed Bug Love

Within my West Street walls,
they built a fire station
in case one of my smokes
torched
their bed bug city

that sprawled across my mattress
where I slept and dreamed
and dreamed about sleeping.

This insect grid gave me love bites
but hey — that's the cost of love
if the love has any worth.

Last night, Liz bugged out.
Over her hot chicken breast, she shot off,
"YOU'RE HAVING A BUG AFFAIR!"
I've held back
that Liz occupied this mattress too.

I never consummated
my bug devotion.
Do you trust me?

Liz forced me
into an Oakland
crawling with rodents
and homeless feet.

Over one block
to 40th and MLK Way,
I swung right and stopped
before a scampering mouse.

"Hey Mouse, how's it going?"

"I'm looking for my mother.
I fear she got trampled by human feet."

"I can't help you. I got human problems."

I scurried down MLK
past a homeless man
sleeping under a money green blanket.

At the West MacArthur intersection,
I halted
before the Bay Bridge Motel.

As I stepped toward the door,
I felt a squish. A bloody bone mess
exposed a dead mouse.
Was this the lost mama mouse?
Nothing could be done

like nothing could be done
for those bed bugs
consumed in the fire
Liz ignited in my ex-backyard.
Did she hear them scream?

In a motel room
stained with blood and bodily fluids,
I spotted a new bed bug district
staring back at me
with their ravenous eyes.

Dentist Revenge

Once Dr. Browning
chewed me out over my flossing failure
at his Geary Street
downtown office,

I decided I wouldn't floss
for the whole breadth
of my birthday month.

I'll celebrate
another swing around the sun
with bloody gums.

At Geary and Kearny, I shamble
past a fountain
dedicated to a statuesque past
I don't care to understand.

With business suit traffic
fumbling by, I spit out blood
onto San Francisco concrete.

Down another block, I glaze
over a homeless man's eyes
gaping into this urban churn.
He isn't a mirror of my future.

Without an address
to house a toothbrush,
this toothless man

sprawls namelessly
before some storefront window's
transparent advertisement.

What's his name?
I should ask
but then I would have to
talk to him.

I just gaze
upon a headless mannequin
minus a brain or teeth or tongue

to push out lies
like the one I assembly-lined
to Dr. Browning:

"Oh I floss every day!
There's something wrong
with my floss. By the way,
can I have a lollipop
on my way out?"

Flirting in the Wild

On a summer weekday in The Dubliner
nestled along West Portal Avenue,
only the regulars churn out
with crinkled bills and sweaty smiles.

At the oaky bar, I call out,
"Hey Sharon, put another Guinness on my tab."
Once Sharon serves me 12oz,
my glass sweats
a River Shannon of condensation

when you spring up,
in your aquamarine shoes
and the Irish flag's tricolors
stretched across your flabby chest,

to parade your potential
across the creaked floor
until you latch onto a female
born in a genus of great ape
now sipping a stout.

Are you any different
than a male blue-footed booby?
Through an oceanside portal,
he displays his luminous

turquoise feet to an avian female
on the rock's edge
of motherhood
where she flaps her independence
in a high tide wash.

You're awash in alcoholic chatter
beside the human female.
Will your romance grow
like a three-leaved shamrock?

Is she your new Irish rose?
Once she displays the diamond
fixed on her ring finger,
you slink back
to your empty stool next to mine.

What can I do?
"Hey Sharon, a shot of Jameson
for my friend right here."

Fatherhood at the Zoo

Squeezed by spectators
at the San Francisco Zoo,
we stand before the outdoor habitat
that houses
a mandrill monkey family.

The crimson noses
of the mother and father, Lulu and Big Joe,
are flanked by denim
blue ridges and golden beards
on muscular bodies. An offspring
springs about in maturing fur.
What vibrancy in simulated nature.

As I hold your young hand —
my paternal blood flows through
all five fingers —
I remember my dad Mark
once took me to this same Zoo
on an October day

where my seven-year-old self
couldn't keep up to his walking
within a foggy stampede of families
not my own.
By the mandrill monkey family,
I shriveled up all alone.

I don't want to be
that kind of dad to you.

In my paternal grasp, you slip away
to step closer, really indulge yourself
on Big Joe's tricolor face
sliding RGB wavelengths
into your eyes' color rods.
Just as fast, your attention scatters.
We scamper away
for a muscled helping of ice cream.

Tomorrow, we'll trek through
a forecast of fog
to Mountain View Cemetery.
At the hill's crest, I'll place a blue orchid
on Grandpa Mark's tombstone.
Tomorrow is his October birthday.

Stray

When a stray bullet
is a stray dog, a stray dog
barks within a chamber of anger

before runaway legs
unhinge themselves
from a gun's steel ownership

to bite an eight-year-old boy's
neck who rides backseat
on an Oakland freeway.

His mother's motherhood
collapses
onto the car floor.

She steers the steel capsule
to a hospital's
bleeding hemorrhage.

I knew this boy as a preschooler:
he smiled inside a classroom's
breathing walls.

Oakland Eyes

Remember when a gun
got found
in a kid's backpack
at our daughter's
elementary school.

As soon as she breathed
back home, I sped over
to feel her heartbeat
vibrate
through my paternal palm.

In a no-sleep dawn,
I hunted for sunrise fear
with my eyes as guns.

Down Telegraph's sidewalk hello,
I needed to place a petal
into the loaded barrel
of my cerulean sight.

When I hunted for sunset joy
with my eyes as seeds,
I spotted a California Wild Rose
blooming within our grass
and concrete neighborhood.

Notes

"In the Smoke": "Remembering the Camp Fire: The deadliest and most destructive wildfire in California's history." CAL FIRE, State of California. fire.ca.gov.

"Watermelon Reveal": Stanchi, Giovanni. *Watermelons, peaches, pears and other fruit in a landscape.* 1645 - 1672. Christie's.

"Flirting in the Wild": Russell, James I. "Where the River Shannon Flows" (1906).

About the Author

Keith Gaboury earned an MFA in Creative Writing from Emerson College. His poems have appeared in such literary publications as *Poetry Quarterly*, *New Millennium Writings*, and the San Francisco Public Library's Poem of the Day Series. The Pedestrian Press published *Oakland, I'm Not Dead* in 2020, Kelsay Books published *The Cosmos is Alive* in 2023, and Falkenberg Press published *Still Human* in 2025. He's also a preschool teacher and a proud bibliophile. Keith lives in Oakland, California. Learn more at keithgaboury.com and keithgaboury.me.

www.ingramcontent.com/pod-product-compliance
Lightning Source LLC
Chambersburg PA
CBHW020327130626
46549CB00003B/1061